Family Communication

A Simple Powerful Communication Strategy to Transform Your Relationship with Your Kids and Enjoy Being a Parent Again

PS: I Owe You!

Thank you for stopping by.

My name is Antony and I am passionate about teaching people literally everything I know about different aspects of life. I am an author and a ghostwriter. I run a small ghostwriting company with slightly over 100 writers. My wife (Faith) and I manage the business along with several other members of the team (editors).

Nice to meet you!

I started publishing (at Fantonpublishers.com) because I'd love to impart the knowledge I gather every single day in my line of work (reading and editing over 10 ghostwritten books every single day). My ghostwriting company deals with literally every topic under the sun, which puts me at a very unique position to learn more in a month than I learnt in my 4 years as a Bachelor of Commerce, Accounting, student. I am constantly answering questions from my friends, relatives and even strangers on various topics that I come across every day at work.

After several years of helping people to achieve different goals (e.g. weight loss, making money online, human resources, management, investing, stress reduction, depression, budgeting, saving etc.) offline thanks to my 'street' as well as 'class' knowledge on different topics, I realized I could be of better help to the world by publishing what I learn. <u>My books</u> are a reflection of what I have been gathering over the years. That's why they are not just focused on one niche but every niche possible out there.

If you would love to be part of my lovely audience who want to change multiple aspects of their life, subscribe to our newsletter <u>http://bit.ly/2fantonpubnewbooks</u> or follow us on social media to receive notifications whenever we publish new books on any niche. You can also send me an email; I would love to hear from you!

PS: Valuable content is my bread and butter. And since I have lots of it to go around, I can share it freely (not everything is about money - **changing lives comes first!**)

I promise; I am busy just as you are and won't spam (I hate spam too)!

Antony,

Website: <u>http://www.fantonpublishers.com/</u>

Email: <u>Support@fantonpublishers.com</u>

Twitter: https://twitter.com/FantonPublisher

Facebook Page:
https://www.facebook.com/Fantonpublisher/

Private Facebook Group For Readers:
https://www.facebook.com/groups/FantonPublishers/

Pinterest: https://www.pinterest.com/fantonpublisher/

Some of the best things in life are free, right?

As a sign of good faith, I will start by giving out content that will help you to implement not only everything I teach in this book but in every other book I write. The content is about life transformation, presented in bit size pieces for easy implementation. I believe that without such a checklist, you are likely to have a hard time implementing anything in this book and any other thing you set out to do religiously and sticking to it for the long haul. It doesn't matter whether your goals relate to weight loss, relationships, personal finance, investing, personal development, improving communication in your family, your overall health, finances, improving your sex life, resolving issues in your relationship, fighting PMS successfully, investing, running a successful business, traveling etc. With a checklist like the one I will show you, you can bet that anything you do will seem a lot easier to implement until the end. This checklist will help you to start well and not lose steam along the way, until the very end.

Therefore, even if you don't continue reading this book, at least read the one thing that will help you in every other aspect of your life.

Send me a message on support@fantonpublishers.com and I will send you my 5 Pillar Life Transformation Checklist.

Your life will never be the same again (if you implement what's in this book), I promise.

Introduction

<u>Don't let ineffective communication break down your family. Discover a creative make your family communication effective so that you can enjoy being a parent!</u>

A huge body of research conducted on happiness and its connection with having a family shows that your family indeed plays a pivotal role in building and sustaining your emotional and psychological well-being.

This means that to be happy in life, you need to have a harmonious and cohesive bond with your family.

While this is extremely important, sometimes it becomes nearly impossible to be around your family especially when you become a parent. **<u>Parenting is certainly a very daunting task- one that requires you to work closely with your kids, understand them, withstand their moods and encourage them to do as you want.</u>**

Although you may feel that it is your kids who do not understand you and are extremely stubborn which is why you have a strained bond with them, it is quite likely that it is your method of dealing with them that is faulty in reality.

Since our happiness is rooted in being around people we absolutely love and care about, and your family does fall in that category, **<u>it is important to improve your</u>**

parenting style so you can build a healthy, loving bond with your kids and together live a happy, beautiful life.

The basis of all healthy, happy relationships is establishing good communication between the people involved. The same rule applies to parenting.

To have a healthy family and a great bond with your children, **focus on improving the way you communicate with them**.

A family lacking healthy communication is like a ship without a rudder. It will flounder even in calm waters and will become dangerously out of control in a storm.

If you are confused on how to do that, this book is precisely what will save your day. This book is **designed to help you transform your bond with your kids by establishing powerful and effective communication with them by simply adopting a few effective techniques.**

With this guide by your side, **you will soon observe a marked improvement in your relationship with your nuclear family, will start feeling happy as well enjoy being a parent.**

More precisely, this book will teach you the following:

- How to identify if you need a change of tact in how you communicate as a family

- **A comprehensive overview of the agile system of family communication**

- How to prepare yourself for change

- **How to build a family brand while following the agile system of family communication**

- How to develop your family's belief board

- **How to build a healthy, loving bond with your kids**

- How to build healthy family rituals

- **How to build a bond of trust with your kids**

- And much, much more!

Without further ado, let's begin this journey to unlocking a happy life with your kids.

I hope you enjoy it!

Table of Contents

If you ever want to succeed at anything, it is very critical that you start with a strong foundation if you really want to increase your odds of emerging successful. Improving your family communication is not any different; you need to start well if you want to realize outstanding results. And starting well in this case is preparing yourself. How do you prepare yourself well for the journey? Well, that's where we will begin our book. Let's begin!

Chapter 1: Prepare Yourself for the Change

To bring a change in your life, (especially a positive one), you need to first prepare yourself for it. Your family especially your kids, are used to living a certain way currently. Although you are trying to do a good thing by trying to build a better bond and communication system with them, it will take time to bring about this change.

During this time, you will experience a few glitches, lots of mood swings and the stubbornness to not agree with what you have in mind by your kids. This is quite normal if it happens because by now, your children have built a certain routine and irrespective of whether it is a good routine or a bad one, it has become a part of their lives. They have become a little set in their ways so it will take you some time, a lot of effort and even more patience to bring about the change you wish to. However, you will achieve your goal and reach the point where you feel happy with your family and they share the same feelings too.

To bring about that change, you need to first prepare yourself for the goal you wish to achieve to ensure you stay strong in the slightly difficult times and do not give up on your intention.

Here's how you can do that.

1: Think About the Change You Want and Be Clear on it

To bring about any positive change, you first need to be clear on what you want. Unless you are very clear on what you wish to achieve, you are quite likely to move forward haphazardly and this will make your life more chaotic.

Think about the change you wish to have in your life as a family and the things you would like to improve on to build a better life. Aren't you happy with your current routine? Do you feel the family members do not support each other in their tasks? Are you unhappy with the way you and your family schedule your tasks because that makes you miss out on important family events? Do you wish to instill certain values in your kids, but somehow are unable to do that? Do you want to teach your children some important life lessons, but somehow you do not have enough time for that? Ponder on all that you are not pleased with currently and would like to change for the better.

Write about the change you wish to bring about as a family and then become determined to achieve it. Create a goal based on it, write it down and then chant it a few times. For instance, you could say, "I am focused on building a healthy, happy bond with my family so all of us understand each other, love each other and support each other" or anything else that resonates with what you have in mind.

Chanting that suggestion helps it settle in your mind and encourages your subconscious mind to embrace it. When your subconscious accepts a suggestion, it makes you more focused on it so you actively work to fulfill that goal.

2: Understand the Importance of a Routine

Once you have more clarity on the goal you would like to achieve, understand that you need to first work on creating a good, healthy and productive routine with your family to achieve that goal. You can only have time for your loved ones, support your kids on their important days and make sure not to miss out on important family events if you have a proper, healthy routine.

If you and your family members have erratic routines, do not plan their tasks, do things just when you feel like and do not talk about your tasks with each other, it is quite likely that you are unaware of the things going on with one another, which is why you have a weak communication system. To improve all of this, you need to build a good, effective routine that is good for the productivity and success of your family. When you understand the importance of having a proper routine, you will easily communicate that importance and your concern to your family as well.

3: Calm and Deep Breathe

Next, you need to train yourself to be calm in stressful times. No matter how much you want, no two people can be exactly the same and it is a rarity that they agree on everything. People are different which is why they have different thoughts, ideas and approaches to doing things. The same applies to your family. Your family is a unit of different individuals that think, feel and behave differently. That being said, this does not mean you cannot function together harmoniously. You can and you will live together as a happy, loving family, but for that to happen, you need to stay calm when the going gets tough.

There will be times when your kids may not agree to what you want instantly, show little to lots of resistance and may even have different ideas to do a certain thing. In such times, you need to stay calm because if you panic and lose your calm, you are likely to strain your bond with your kids. Staying calm helps you focus on the important things, get better perspective on things and analyze them nonjudgmentally. This helps you reach better conclusions and make sound decisions.

For that to happen, make a habit to practice deep breathing. Sit somewhere peaceful and gently bring your attention on to your breath. Observe how you inhale and exhale for a few moments and when you feel calmer, inhale deeply through your nose to a count of 5. Next, hold that breathe to another count of 5 and exhale it with force through your mouth to a final count of 5. Do that for about 10 times and you will feel more peaceful than before.

Once you build a habit of deep breathing, build another of practicing it just when you feel stressed. If your child comes up with a new idea or does not agree with a system you are trying to incorporate in the routine or is being stubborn, take a few deep breaths and relax. When you feel calmer, you will start thinking about the issue at hand rationally and may come up with unique ideas to resolve it. That's what good parenting is about.

Now that we have covered the basics, let us move on to the first step of building a happy family. The next chapter covers it in detail.

Chapter 2: Follow the Agile System of Parenting

Often, frustrations and a lack of love and warmth stem from a lack of a proper, healthy and effective routine. If you as a family are unaware of each other's routine and you do not pay attention to your kids' needs when creating a family plan, you are likely to have problems with your kids.

A lack of proper planning and an effective routine is why you see chaos all around you. Children running here and there aimlessly, frustrations rising every minute; and lots of tasks marked as pending are all the results of not having an effective routine. If you can relate to this, this explains why you have stopped enjoying being a parent. The solution to your problem is to adopt an agile system.

Understanding an Agile System

An agile system is an approach to doing your work in a more efficient and effective manner. This requires you to divide the family into two or more teams and dividing your tasks into small chunks as well. You schedule your tasks for the day or the week keeping everyone's priorities in mind and try to come up with a schedule wherein everyone's needs are considered. The focus lies on ideas flowing all the way up from the bottom and not from the top down. So even if your youngest kid gives you an idea, you consider it and if makes sense to you, you adopt it. This way, everyone gets to have their say in setting a family schedule and nobody feels unheard or unimportant.

Not only that, but this system also requires you to constantly review your progress and the schedule so you make adjustments to the plan as you move forward. If something urgent comes up or you feel a certain task or idea has lost its importance with time, you include or eliminate it, respectively.

The agile system has helped many families move from insanity and sanity and reclaim their happiness. This approach not only helps you do stuff together as a family and make sure you do not miss out on each other's important events, but also improves the communication gap created earlier on between you and your family. When you, your partner/ spouse and kids sit together to discuss a suitable plan, you talk to each other, give everyone a chance to speak and listen to one another. This helps you understand each other and build a better bond.

The Agile System is based on the following key points:

1. **There is Always a Solution to a Problem**: Family conflicts can be hard and can make you feel that there is no way you can be together as a family. Even if you have small kids, if you do not have a proper routine and haven't planned things properly, you are likely to find your life extremely chaotic, disturbing and annoying. Even though you wish to find pleasure in

raising your kids, you are quite likely to hate it with all the mayhem going on around you and this may make you feel that there is no solution to your problem. There is always a solution to any issues and all the problems in the world come with a fix and so does a chaotic routine and parenting, and the solution to that is to follow an agile system. When adopting this approach, bear in mind that you must always focus on finding solutions to your problems so you become solution-focused and not problem-focused. This way, you train your mind to get deeper into things and find a way out of a problem and not let yourself get lost in it.

2. **Your Kids Need to be Empowered:** Most of the time, we as parents, feel that we ought to make decisions for our kids and if we do not do that, they are likely to make poor decisions for themselves. To help them out in life and to make sure they live a good life, we make all the decisions for them and that then makes them dependent on us for a long time. So when they grow up and we ask them to do their tasks on their own, they are quite likely to refuse and keep being dependent on us. This increases our workload making it difficult for us to manage everything on our own. This issue can be easily resolved with the help of the agile system. The agile system requires you to teach your kids executive skills by empowering them. You allow them to play a big role in upbringing

themselves by letting them plan their own schedule, create weekly goals, make their to-do lists, suggest ideas and see what works for them. When you let your children do their own work and plan their routine on their own, you make them accountable for their actions and train them to be independent. This way, they learn to do their tasks on their own as well as be responsible for the decisions they make and not come running to you with complains. So when you start adopting the agile system, you need to slowly empower your children to do things on their own, plan their own schedules, create their daily and weekly routine and figure out for themselves what works for them.

3. **You are not Perfect when it Comes to Parenting and that's Okay**: Another important rule of the agile manifesto is that you can never be a perfect parent and that is perfectly fine. Perfectionism is a myth and nobody can ever be perfect so it is best not to pursue it and settle for good enough instead. Although you wish to take great decisions always, have a chaos-free house and kids who never throw tantrums, this is not always possible. You wish to be an all-knowing parent, but no matter how you try, this can never be possible because when you start to pry too much into your kids' lives, they feel their privacy is being compromised and this could easily create a rift between you and them. To keep that from happening,

go easy on yourself and your kids and try to create a good communication system between you and your kids. Stop focusing too much on being the perfect parent or having everything done perfectly. Once you eliminate that concern, you start going more with the flow and go easy on yourself. When you start taking it easy and focus more on planning stuff as well as communicating things with your kids, you involve the entire family in the plan and create a breathable and effective routine for the family.

4. **Flexibility is Important**: Also, understand that you need to have a flexible mindset when you work on adopting an agile system. Being flexible helps you easily make changes to the routine when needed. When you are flexible, you evaluate the schedule on a regular basis, make changes to it as needed and then adapt to the change. This way, you keep assessing your routine to make sure you keep moving forward smoothly and then bring necessary changes to it accordingly that only improve your efficiency and productivity as a family.

To make life easier for yourself as a parent and for your family altogether, you need to follow these rules of the agile system and imbed them in your mind. **Once you accept them, start working on the following guidelines.**

1: Have a Pep Talk with Your Family

Just as you prepared yourself for the change, you need to do the same with your kids. Gather them in the family room and talk to them about how you wish to have a more meaningful relationship with them. Start off with how much you love and care about them. Say a few nice things about every family member to shower your affection on to them. This improves their mood and makes them to have positive feelings towards you.

Once you feel positivity in their attitude towards you, talk about how your current routine lacks structure and how it keeps all of you from living better, meaningful lives. Next, talk about the agile system and how it can help you live efficiently and effectively. Kids usually learn and understand things better with examples so tell them a few examples of how adopting the agile system can benefit them and improve their individual life for the better as well. For instance, once they learn to follow and implement it successfully, they can use it to schedule their plans with friends and school activities to live harmoniously.

If any of your kids show resistance to the idea, give him/ her some time to come to terms with it and absorb the new idea. As stated before, things are not going to be as simple as you expect them to be. There will be rough patches, but you have to stay strong so take a few deep breaths every time you experience some resistance by a family member to calm yourself down. That being said, do not budge from your stance and keep talking about the agile system every now and then. Soon enough, your kids are likely to give in to your commitment and agree to follow it.

2: Create a Weekly Schedule Together

Once you feel everyone is on the same page, start off by creating a weekly schedule together. Ask everyone to create a list of their most important tasks and write them on post-its. Take a couple of hours to complete this task. When everyone has a list or lists of their own, go through them slowly and then create a schedule for everyone that suits the family as a whole.

Ask everyone to find his or her high priority tasks from the list and when they wish for each task to be done. Go through all the tasks back and forth to come up with a schedule that suits everyone and does not compromise on anyone's high priority tasks. Once the list is ready, take a calendar and put all the tasks for the week in it.

In addition, also create a morning, afternoon and night time checklists for your kids so they know the different small tasks they need to do and make sure to follow through with them. Tasks like taking your medicine/ vitamins on time, taking a shower, eating breakfast, combing hair, dressing up, finishing lunch, going to football practice, changing clothes at night etc. could be put on that checklist.

You along with all your family members need to go through the calendar with your tasks and schedule every morning before or after breakfast to make sure you have the right schedule with you. Also, check off any task that has been completed and ask everyone if they need to move another task to the front or replace it with some other task or eliminate a certain task altogether. Things and priorities keep on changing and it is important to revisit your schedule time and again to ensure you are on the right track.

3: Break Tasks into Smaller, Doable Parts

To make it easier for your kids to do their chores, encourage them to break the task into smaller tasks and then work on every part one by one. Also known as the 'Pomodoro Technique', this easy-to-follow time management technique makes it easier for you to work on a rather large and overwhelming task and quickly get done with it. When you have a task divided into smaller, more manageable parts, you get started with it easily and adjust into it smoothly too.

4: Follow the 30 to 60 Second Tip

This is an extremely effective tip that helps you and your family members stay on the right track when following your schedule. You are supposed to get started with a chore and then glance at your to-do list or schedule after every 30 to 60 seconds especially once you are done with a task. This helps you ensure you are on the right track and do not go off the track and engage into a meaningless task when you are supposed to work on something important.

Not only do you need to conform to this rule, you need to ask your kids to do the same. Just guide them about this rule and encourage them to follow it as it helps them stay on track and work efficiently. This way, you will help them stay in charge of their own routine and won't have to keep an eye on them every few hours. Also, you won't have to be the bad guy in the equation since they will be the ones managing their routine.

5: Make Kanban Lists

A kanban list is a Japanese list that contains vertical columns corresponding to the different tasks and their nature. Usually, it contains 3 columns: to do, working/ doing and done. You go through your calendar and put the different tasks for the day in a Kanban list for the day. Those that you have yet to work on go in the 'to do' column; those that you are working on or your work-in-progress go under the 'doing' category; and all the tasks that you are done with go in the 'done' column. This way, you easily keep track of your performance and know what you are supposed to do. You can create other types of columns and lists in a Kanban list as well. Here are some examples of Kanban lists.

	Monday	Tuesday	Wednesday	Thursday	Friday
Comb Hair	Done				
Wash Face	Done				
Take Breakfast	Done				
Change Clothes	Done				

Ask your kids to follow a kanban list every day so they stay aware of their important chores and make sure to attend to the work-in-progress and the to-do ones right after they have finished a few chores.

6: Have a Weekly Family Meeting

At the end of every week, make sure you have a detailed family meeting. Schedule that meeting at a time that is convenient for everyone so all the family members can make time for the meeting and can be a part of it. This is a good tip especially if you have kids older than 6 who have different activities and even plans outside of home.

Start the meeting on a positive note and thank everyone, especially your kids, for being a part of it. Next, go through the schedule of the past week and ask everyone the three questions below, one by one:

- **How did the week go and what went really well?** This question gives insight into how that week went for each one of the family members and anything that went really well for them and was considered as an accomplishment by them. Everyone gets to share their experiences and little to big achievements, which only brings all of you closer as a family. For instance, your daughter may have had a nice week because she did all her tasks on time and since she had planned things earlier, she may have gotten to her lacrosse practices on time as well which helped her perform better. Make sure to appreciate everyone for his or her hard work and especially for the accomplishments. Hug your kids and partner/ spouse, say nice things to them and even plan a little treat to celebrate their accomplishments. You could go out to eat something, watch a movie or do anything else that fits your schedule for the day. The idea is just to do something pleasant together as a family and be a part of each other's little victories because being there for one another and supporting each other as a family is what brings families together and precisely what your family has been missing out on. A major reason why you stopped having fun as a parent is because you were missing out on the essence of parenthood- being there for your kids and being a part of their accomplishments. A lot of it was rooted in not having a routine that suits everyone, which is why all of you kept doing your own stuff and could never really work as a unit. However, things are changing for the better now allowing you to be there for each other and this helps you bond better with your kids.

- **What did not go so well or as planned?** Although a schedule does help smooth out things, sometimes things may not go as planned. Also, since you have just started implementing an agile system, you and your family are likely to have a few glitches down the road. Although you did communicate everything together when setting the schedule, a few tasks could have overlapped and you may have had to take the car when it was time for your partner to use it; or a certain time of the day may not have been suitable for your son to do a certain task; or your kids may have found it difficult to do 3 high priority tasks in a day and maybe they want to go slow. There could be a million things that may not have gone nicely for your family and you can only find that out if you talk to each other and share your experiences. So ask everyone about what did not go as planned during the week and what in their opinion could have actually helped them. Share your insights with each other and make sure to comfort your kids when they share their unfortunate experiences with you instead of being harsh on them. Often saying things like 'Oh, you made a mistake again!' or 'Can't you be more responsible' are enough to sabotage your child's self-esteem and make him/her lose his/her faith in you. Instead of using such suggestions, be kind and supportive to your kids and say things such as, *'I am sad that things did not go as planned for you, but it is okay. Unfortunate things happen at times and they only help us learn. I am so proud of you that you handled that experience strongly and are now discussing it with us.'* Loving and kind words by parents are often the only thing kids really want to hear so if you give them your support, they will feel happy and light.

- **What do we want to work on in the following week?** Next, ask everyone about their plans for the coming week and how do they wish to work in it. Ask them about the tasks they would like to accomplish in the next week and any strategies they have in mind to improve on the mistakes made this week so they can be more productive. Ask everyone to write down his or her stuff on post-its again and go through everything one by one to create a more effective schedule for the following week.

Once you have gone through everything, wrap up the meeting on a good note and wish everyone good luck for the next week. It is important to stick to these guidelines and follow them consistently week after week. The more you practice them, the better you get hang of the strategies and improve on them. This improves your efficiency and productivity as a family and together, you have fun doing all your tasks.

Bruce Feiler created the agile system and he and his family have benefitted greatly from the technique. When they started adopting this system, they were soon able to move out of a chaotic routine to a smoother and more effective one. This made life a lot easier and manageable for them and he and his wife started having fun being parents again. You too can bring back joy into your life and make it more beautiful than ever by simply following the agile system.

In addition to doing that, you also need to focus on incorporating certain values in your family and making sure you raise your kids the way you want to. For that, you must set your family's brand and work as a family to maintain that. The next chapter talks about it in detail.

Chapter 3: Build Your Family Brand

A family brand is just like a product brand. When a product is launched, the company wishes for everyone to know about the brand and then promotes it a certain way to maintain the brand image of the product. If an energy drink is portrayed to give you a big boost of energy so you can take on any sort of adventure and never shy away from anything, the company will create all the advertisements of that drink based on that theme. This is what helps the company build a particular brand image of the product.

When you go out in social situations, meet people and even when meeting other parents, you would want everyone to perceive you as a certain family that is known for certain qualities. For instance, if honesty is an important value to you, you would want everyone to see you and your family as a bunch of honest people who are dedicated to their work and family and never lie to one another. Similarly, if you have any other value that you wish to impart to your family members and want others to know you for it, you would focus on creating that brand for your family.

A family brand is precisely what you need to build for everyone to form a certain perception of your family. Moreover, having a family brand also gives you clarity on what values and lessons you wish to teach your children so you and your spouse together work on that goal and build a healthy and happy family.

Bruce Feiler learned about building a family brand from his friend David Kiddler. He saw that the Kiddler family had a family belief board that comprised of certain values they wanted their family to focus on and that is how together they created their family brand. This helped the Feiler family create their own family brand and mission statement as well which was: "May your first word be adventure and your last word be love," This helped Bruce Feiler and his wife realize that they wanted to have their family brand based on adventure and love. This also helped them build their life a certain way and focus only on things that bring them true value and happiness.

Here is how you can create your own family brand.

Create Your Family's Belief Board

First, you need to create your family's belief board, which is a list of all the things you and your family believe in and the vision you have for your family. This helps you and your kids understand your family's goal better and makes it easier for you to stick to it. When something is written down and is visible to you instead of being just in your hcad, it naturally becomes easier to digest and implement it.

Here is how you can create your family's belief board.

1: Understand Your Core Values

If your kids are too young to understand what core values are and get in on this discussion, you can have it with your partner/spouse only. However, if they are above 3 and you wish for them to play an important role in the discussion, do it with them. You may need to go over certain things several times to make them clearer to your children, but trust me, you will have a lot of fun together as a family.

Ask everyone to join in on a pajama party and have an interesting discussion over your family's favorite food or snacks. Ask everyone to think of his or her core values and the principles they want the family to work on together so they build a certain family brand.

Here are some core values you should consider to decide what works best for your family.

- Dependability

- Loyalty

- Reliability

- Love

- Commitment

- Consistency

- Honesty

- Compassion

- Positivity

- Growth
- Open-mindedness
- Creativity
- Innovation
- Passion
- Adventurous
- Efficiency
- Good humor
- Motivation
- Fitness
- Respect
- Education
- Patriotism
- Trust
- Being Religious
- Courage
- Perseverance
- Humanity

- Environmentalism

- Loving

Go through these and different values one by one to figure out which values align with your core values and beliefs. Take 5 to 10 values and then focus on them to create your core values. Also, think of the things you would like to do and wish for your kids to be involved in and understand to come up with the right set of core values.

Once you are through with this step, figure out your vision for your family and create your mission statement.

2: Find Your Vision and Mission

To build a clearer and good brand- one that aligns with what you have in mind for your family and how you wish for your family to be perceived by others, it is important to have a clear vision and mission for your family.

To have a good mission, you need to think about the vision first. How is it that you see your family as a unit and what is it that you wish for your family to do together, be known for and follow in life? Do you plan for your family to have its own family business that everyone is a part of? Or do you wish for everyone to be close to each other, but do whatever they want independently? Or do you wish for everyone to follow a more individualistic approach to living their lives? Or do you want a closely knit family that is not dependent on each other, but makes sure to get each other's consent, support and blessings before embarking on different ventures?

Ask yourself these questions and ask your partner/spouse and kids to do the same so everyone gets a chance to share their views and give their input in this important decision. You need to have a clear vision to create a good and meaningful mission. When you have clarity on your vision, move on to creating your family mission and then use it to craft your mission statement. Whatever your vision is, think about how you wish to follow through with it and achieve it and then use that knowledge to create your mission. For instance, if you want a loving family where members support each other and where members are honest as well as loyal to each other, think about how you could bring about that result. For instance, if you focus on being around each other every day and spending quality time with one another, you could achieve that goal so maybe your family's mission statement could be: 'Spend quality time with one another and stay united.'

Make sure to consider the strengths, weaknesses, likes, dislikes and passions of each family member when creating the vision and mission. It is important to consider everyone before making this important decision so you are fair to every member. It takes a little time to create your family's vision and mission so be patient with yourself and your partner/spouse and kids if they are involved in this process. Once you have clarity on your vision and mission, write it down and then add it to your family's beliefs board along with your core values.

The family's beliefs board can be a decorative piece of art that you can put in your family room and glance at from time to time to stay on the right track. You could take a canvas, paint some images on it and write the core values and mission statement on it. You could ask the kids to add some decorative ornaments to it to beautify it and then put it up on a prominent wall of the room. This way, you will engage your kids in a healthy activity and will also make them a part of the overall process.

Once you are clearer on the values you wish for your kids to learn, it is now time to work on building those. The next chapter shares with you some powerful ideas to do just that.

Chapter 4: Work on Building a Healthy, Loving Bond with Your Kids

Building a good bond with your kids is extremely important to bring them closer to you and to feel happy being a parent. Here are some powerful ways to achieve that goal. Not only will these methods improve your relationship with your children, they will also help you fulfill your vision for the family as a whole.

Build Healthy Family Rituals

A ritual is anything that you do on a regular basis, be it daily, weekly or monthly. A family ritual is a ritual that you carry out with your family. It is important to have a few healthy and fun family rituals so you and your family spend some quality time together, get to know each other better, come closer to each other, do fun activities as a unit and build beautiful memories as one, happy family. For instance, if you watch a movie together every Saturday night and order pizza, you turn this activity into a weekly ritual. This way, you get to spend some fun and relaxing time together and be in each other's company without doing anything mentally or physically taxing.

Here are some great ideas for family rituals that not only help you spend a great time together as a family, but also help instill different values in your kids.

1: Do Fun Things Together

There needs to be one family ritual wherein all of you spend quality time over a fun, relaxing activity. It could be anything that helps unwind all of you and gives you a break from the monotonous and exhausting routine. You could watch a movie together, go on a nice picnic, do water fights, play tag, go to an amusement park or do anything fun every week that gives you all a good break and opportunity to have nice laughs in the company of one another.

Make sure to ask every family member about his/her idea of something fun. There are kids who find going to the museum fun and if even one of your kids enjoys that or something similar that may be considered as boring by the other family members, do not ignore it. You could make it a monthly or biweekly thing, but you need to consider everyone's wishes and respect them by opting them.

2: Read Together

Reading is a great habit to instill in your kids. As Dr. Seuss said, *'The more you read, the more you know and the more you know, the more places you go.'* If you want your kids to turn into smart, confident and creative adults, help them build the habit of reading from a young age.

Although it is best to read as a family daily, if you cannot make this a daily ritual, do it at least 3 to 4 days a week. You could all take turns reading a page or two of your favorite book or maybe a whole story (short stories for kids) to the entire family; or you could pick one storybook that everyone loves and read out to your kids. You could ask your kids to pick out their favorite stories over the weekend and then read one book a day to them at night or any other time of the day that suits you.

In addition, you could have a little kid's story telling sessions when one of your kids shares his/her favorite story with the entire family. Make sure to ask your kid(s) what he/she learned from the story and share your input as well. Also, you could ask your kids to go through the story once again when you are done reading it. This reinforces their knowledge about the story and improves their memory.

Moreover, pick stories on subjects and lessons that you wish to teach your kids. If you want your kids to be courageous and strong as these are your core family views, read stories to them based on these values. Similarly, if you wish for them to listen to their heart and do what they want to in life, choose any story or book that is created on that theme.

3: Do Something Healthy

It is important to teach your kids the importance of being healthy, physically, emotionally and psychologically. Building a healthy ritual is a good way to do that. Think of any healthy activity that you could do together as a family that improves your health. You could go for a quick walk or a jog every evening; do yoga; play a sport; practice deep breathing; and even meditate together.

Moreover, ensure to eat one healthy meal together in the day. It could be any meal that you can have together, be it breakfast, lunch or dinner and that meal must be really healthy comprising of fresh fruits, vegetables, nuts, seeds, lean meat cuts and organic goods. This teaches your kids the importance of eating nutritious food and gives you a chance to all of you to do that together.

4: Talk to Each Other

As important as it is to do healthy, enjoyable and meaningful things together, it is equally important to talk to your kids and partner/spouse when spending quality time together. Make sure to spend a little time with one another daily when you ask each other about their day, what went wrong or good, any issues they had during the day or any significant experience they would like to talk about.

Also, make it a point to talk about your family history and childhood of both your spouse/partner and yourself with your kids. You could tell them fun and exciting stories about your childhood and share your memorable, both good and bad, moments with them. This draws them closer to you and increases their interest in your family background.

5: Just Relax

There needs to be a time that all of you spend together doing nothing significant and only relaxing. Set a time of the day or a day of the week when all of you just lie down together and relax. Being in each other's presence without actually doing something helps you build a bond that does not need to rely on any activity. There will be times in your life when you do not wish to do something or for someone to say something to you, but only be around you to make you feel better. Relaxing with your family helps you build that understanding with your family so they know how to calm you down without uttering a word.

6: Support One Another

If any of your kids is in a music band, part of a sports team or involved in any activity that has some public events or sessions, do join them in to support them. For instance, you could go to your son's football game or your daughter's guitar lessons to let them know you support of their activities. This encourages them to pursue what they want and makes them aware of your care.

7: Visit Family

Do visit your relatives together as a family frequently, preferably on special occasions. You could do Thanksgiving with your parents and Christmas with your spouse's parents or as it works for both of you, but do teach your kids the importance of being around family and loving them by visiting them as often as it is possible for you.

8: Take Input from Your Kids before Making any Important Family Decisions

If your kids have reached a sensible age, mostly 7+ years, make sure to include them in on any discussion relevant to important family decisions. Whether you are planning to move to a new city, change your house, host a party at home or buy a pet, make sure to talk to your kids about the idea and get their input on it as well. Your kids need to feel they are a part of the family and that their suggestion is important to you so they feel more included in the family.

Also, when you do take a suggestion from your kids, do not discard it instantly thinking a young mind gave it to you. Instead, thank your kid for the important input, discuss it with your spouse, analyze it and implement it if you feel it could be beneficial for all of you then make sure to thank them again for a great advice.

You do not need to work on all these ideas instantly- take one or two and slowly build a habit of them. As you become more accustomed to those practices, add in some new rituals so all of you hang out more often as a family.

Moreover, you need to work on winning the trust of your kids so they learn to trust you and share their problems with you. The next chapter discusses how to do that.

Chapter 5: Building a Bond of Trust with Your Kids

Your kids need to know that they can trust you and share their personal stuff with you. If you do not build a bond of trust with your kids, they are quite likely not to share their personal and important or even unfortunate experiences with you and may become victimized by issues such as abuse, bullying and emotional problems.

Here is how you can build a healthy bond with your kids so they know you trust them and that they too trust you equally.

1: Respect Your Child and His Ideas

Your child needs to know that you love and respect him/her and that you will not be judgmental of his/her ideas. This is how he/she will learn to slowly trust you and share his/her important experiences with you and your spouse/partner.

Whenever any of your kids comes to both of you, or one parent individually to discuss something, do not judge him/her. If he/she breaks some important news to you, do not let them feel that you do not appreciate or accept the idea even if it feels weird or inappropriate to you. You need to love your kid for whom he/ she is and that's how you will build a good bond with him/ her. For that, it is important to overcome any of your fears and let go of your biased beliefs that keep you from loving and trusting your kids.

2: Give Your Child a Chance to Speak

Whenever your child comes to you with a story or an idea, do not cut him/her out. Let him/her finish what he/she has to say and when he/she has poured his/her heart out, share your ideas with him/her. Listen to your child with full attention and do not fidget with stuff or make weird facial expressions when listening to him/her so he/ she knows he/she has your attention and that you love him/her.

3: Make Your Child Feel Comfortable

Some children experience abuse, bullying and other unfortunate experiences too. As much as you do not want for your child to go through these issues, there is a chance he/she may be suffering from them.

To find that out, get a better understanding of your child's routines and activities without prying on him/her. Ask your children from time to time of their whereabouts, any new activities they are engaged in, any new friends they have made or any new ideas they have. Next, pay attention to their behavior and if you notice anything suspicious, talk to them without making them feel uncomfortable.

Do not jump to a conclusion instantly; instead, ask your child if everything is okay with him/her and if he/she assures you there is nothing to worry about, do not push him/her further. You can then share any of your unfortunate experiences with him/her after a few days to encourage him/her to open up to you. If they do tell you about any unfortunate experience or issue they are going through, listen to it patiently and ask them about how they would like to follow through with the problem. You must take any ideas they have into account and then do what you feel is best as their parent. This way, they learn to trust you better and feel comfortable around you.

In addition to working on all these ideas, set a few rules and regulations that you ask the entire family to abide by so your kids know there are certain principles they need to follow and stick to it. This brings in more structure into the family routine and helps things progress smoothly.

Conclusion

We have come to the end of the book. Thank you for reading and congratulations for reading until the end.

I hope this book offered you the value you were looking for and helps you regain the sanity you were missing in your family for a long time.

Now is your turn to take action!

Do You Like My Book & Approach To Publishing?

If you like my writing and style and would love the ease of learning literally everything you can get your hands on from Fantonpublishers.com, I'd really need you to do me either of the following favors.

6 Things

I'll be honest; publishing books on what I learn in my line of work gives me satisfaction. But the biggest satisfaction that I can get as an author is knowing that I am influencing people's lives positively through the content I publish. Greater joy even comes from knowing that customers appreciate the great content that they have read in every book through giving feedback, subscribing to my newsletter, sending emails to tell me how transformative the content they read is, following me on social media and buying several of my books. That's why I am always seeking to engage my readers at a personal level to know them and for them to know me, not just as an author but as a person because we all want to belong. That's why I strive to use different channels to engage my readers so that I can ultimately build a cordial relationship with them for our mutual success i.e. I succeed as an author while at the same time my readers learn stuff that takes days and sometimes weeks to write, edit, format and publish in a matter of hours.

To build this relationship, I'd really appreciate if you could do any or all the following:

1: First, I'd Love It If You Leave a Review of This Book on Amazon.

Let me be honest; reviews play a monumental role in determining whether customers purchase different products online. From the thousands of other books that are on Amazon about the topic, you chose to read this one. I am grateful for that. I may not know why you read my book, especially until the end considering the fact that most readers don't read until the end. Perhaps you purchased this book after reading some of the reviews and were glued with reading the book because it was educative and engaging. Even if you didn't read it because of the positive reviews, perhaps you can make the next customer's purchasing decision a lot easier by posting a review of this book on Amazon!

I'd love it if you did that, as this would help me spread word out about my books and publishing business. The more the readers, the bigger a community we build and we all benefit! If you could leave your honest review of this book on Amazon, I'd be forever grateful (well, I am already grateful to you for purchasing the book and reading it until the end- I don't' take that for granted!). Please Leave a Review of This Book on Amazon.

2: <u>**Check Out My Other Books**</u>

As I stated earlier, my biggest joy in all this is building an audience that loves my approach to publishing and the amazing content I publish. I know every author has his/her style. Mine is publishing what I learn to readers out there so that they can learn what is trending, what other readers are also searching for in the nonfiction world and much more. As such, if you <u>read the other books I have published</u>, you will undoubtedly know a lot more than the average person on a diverse range of issues. And as you well know, knowledge is power- and the biggest investment that you can ever have on your life!

PS: If you want me to filter everything for you to include only Ketogenic diet books, you can <u>subscribe to my newsletter</u> and I will send you a list of all my Ketogenic diet books along with other useful content that I come across to ensure you succeed while at it <u>http://bit.ly/2Cketodietfanton</u>.

3: **Let's Get In Touch**

Let's get closer than just leaving reviews and buying my other books. Reach out to me through email, like or follow me on social media and let's interact. You will perhaps get to know stuff about me that will change your life in a way. As we interact, we will also influence each other in a way. I' definitely would love to learn something from you as we get to know each other.

Antony

Website: http://www.fantonpublishers.com/

Email: Support@fantonpublishers.com

Twitter: https://twitter.com/FantonPublisher

Facebook **Page**: https://www.facebook.com/Fantonpublisher/

My Ketogenic Diet Books Page: https://www.facebook.com/pg/Fast-Keto-Meals-336338180266944

Private Facebook Group For Readers: https://www.facebook.com/groups/FantonPublishers/

Pinterest: https://www.pinterest.com/fantonpublisher/

4: Grab Some Freebies On Your Way Out; Giving Is Receiving, Right?

I gave you 2 freebies at the start of the book, one on general life transformation and one about the Ketogenic diet. You are free to choose either or both!

Ketogenic Diet Freebie: http://bit.ly/2fantonpubketo

5 Pillar Life Transformation Checklist: http://bit.ly/2fantonfreebie

5: Suggest Topics That You'd Love Me To Cover To Increase Your Knowledge Bank.

As I stated, I love feedback; any type of feedback- positive or negative. As such, make sure to reach out. I am looking forward to seeing your suggestions and insights on the topic. You could even suggest improvements to this book. Simply send me a message on Support@fantonpublishers.com. As a publisher, I strive to publish content that my readers are actively looking for. Therefore, your input is highly important.

6: Subscribe To My Newsletter To Know When I Publish New Books.

I already mentioned this earlier; I love to connect with my readers. This is just another avenue for me to connect to you. As such, if you would love to know whenever I publish new books and blog posts, subscribe to my newsletter at http://bit.ly/2fantonpubnewbooks. You will be the first to know whenever I have fresh content!

My Other Books

As I already mentioned, I write books on all manner of topics. In this part of the book, I have categorized them all for easy reading. If you wish to receive notifications about a certain category of books, I have provided a link below every category to ensure you only receive what you are looking for.

Weight Loss Books

You can search for the titles on Amazon.

General Weight Loss Books

The books in this category will help you lose weight irrespective of the approach you are using i.e. dieting or workout. I recommend you have them even if you are on specific diets or using specific workouts for weight loss.

Binge Eating: Binge Eating Disorder Cure: Easy To Follow Tips For Eating Only What Your Body Needs

Lose Weight: Lose Weight Fast Naturally: How to Lose Weight Fast Without Having To Become a Gym Rat or Dieting Like a Maniac

Lose Weight: Lose Weight Permanently: Effective Strategies on How to Lose Weight Easily and Permanently

Get updates when we publish any book about weight loss: http://bit.ly/2fantonweightlossbooks

Weight Loss Books On Specific Diets

Ketogenic Diet Books

KETOGENIC DIET: Keto Diet Made Easy: Beginners Guide on How to Burn Fat Fast With the Keto Diet (Including 100+ Recipes That You Can Prepare Within 20 Minutes)- New Edition

KETOGENIC DIET: Ketogenic Diet Recipes That You Can Prepare Using 7 Ingredients and Less in Less Than 30 Minutes

Ketogenic Diet: Lose Weight Rapidly With Paleo Friendly Ketogenic Diet Recipes You Can Make Within 25 Minutes

Get updates when we publish any book on the Ketogenic diet: http://bit.ly/2fantonpubketo

Intermittent Fasting Books

Get updates when we publish any book on intermittent fasting: http://bit.ly/2fantonbooksIF

Any Other Diet

Get updates when we publish any book on any other diet that will help you to lose weight and keep it off: http://bit.ly/2fantonsdietbooks

Relationships Books

<u>Wedding: Budget Wedding: Wedding Planning On The Cheap (Master How To Plan A Dream Wedding On Budget)</u>

<u>How To Get Your Ex Back: Step By Step Formula On How To Get Your Ex Back And Keep Him/her For Good</u>

<u>SEX POSITIONS: Sex: Unleash The Tiger In You Using These 90-Day Sex Positions With Pictures</u>

<u>Money Problems: How To Solve Relationship Money Problems: Save Your Marriage By Learning How To Fix All Your Money Problems And Save Your Relationship</u>

Get updates when we publish any book that will help you improve on your personal and professional relationships: http://bit.ly/2fantonsrelations

Personal Development

<u>Body Language: Master Body Language: A Practical Guide to Understanding Nonverbal Communication and Improving Your Relationships</u>

Get updates when we publish any book that will help you become a better person by boosting your productivity, achieving more of your goals, beating procrastination, breaking bad habits, forming new habits, beat stress, building your self-esteem and confidence and much more: http://bit.ly/2fantonpubpersonaldevl

Personal Finance & Investing Books

Real Estate: Rental Property Investment Guide: How To Buy & Manage Rental Property For Profits

MONEY: Make Money Online: 150+ Real Ways to Make Real Money Online (Plus 50 Bonus Tips to Guarantee Your Success)

Money: How To Make Money Online: Make Money Online In 101 Ways

Get updates when we publish any book that will help you up your game in personal finance and investing: http://bit.ly/2fantonpersfinbooks

Health & Fitness Books

PMS CURE: Easy To Follow Home Remedies For PMS & PMDD

Testosterone: How to Boost Your Testosterone Levels in 15 Different Ways Naturally

<u>**Hair Loss: How to Stop Hair Loss: Actionable Steps to Stop Hair Loss (Hair Loss Cure, Hair Care, Natural Hair Loss Cures)**</u>

Get updates when we publish any book that will help you up your game in health and fitness: http://bit.ly/2fantonhealthnfit

Book Summaries

This category will feature summaries of some of your favorite books, written in a manner you can easily digest and follow:

<u>**Summary: The Millionaire Next Door: The Surprising Secrets of America's Wealthy**</u>

Get updates whenever we publish new book summaries: http://bit.ly/2fantons

All The Other Niches

This category of books includes anything that we cannot realistically fit in the categories above. As always, if you want just about anything you can get to read, this is the category for you!

Travel Books

<u>**Kenya: Travel Guide: The Traveler's Guide to Make The Most Out of Your Trip to Kenya (Kenya Tourists Guide)**</u>

World Issues Books

ISIS/ISIL: The Rise and Rise of the Islamic State: A Comprehensive Guide on ISIS & ISIL

Get notifications when we publish books on anything else above from the niches I mentioned above: http://bit.ly/2fantonpubnewbooks

See You On The Other Side!

See, I publish books on just about any topic imaginable!

If you have any suggestions on topics you would want me to cover, feel free to get in touch:

Website: http://www.fantonpublishers.com/

Email: Support@fantonpublishers.com

Twitter: https://twitter.com/FantonPublisher

My Ketogenic Diet Books Page: https://www.facebook.com/pg/Fast-Keto-Meals-336338180266944

Facebook Page: https://www.facebook.com/Fantonpublisher/

Private Facebook Group For Readers: https://www.facebook.com/groups/FantonPublishers/

Pinterest: https://www.pinterest.com/fantonpublisher/

PS: You can subscribe to my mailing list to know when I publish new books:

Hey! This is not the entire list! You can check an updated list of all my books on:

My **Author** **Central**:
amazon.com/author/fantonpublishers

My Website: http://www.fantonpublishers.com

Stay With Me On My Journey To Making Passive Income Online

I have to admit; my writing business makes several six figures a year in profits (after paying ourselves salaries). Until recently, I didn't realize just how hard we worked to build this business to what it has become so far.

However, while it is profitable and I want to do it in the long term, I understand its limitations. I know I cannot have an endless number of writers at a time especially if we are to continue delivering high quality products to our customers and readers consistently.

That's why I have recently started getting more serious with self-publishing to help me build a passive income business i.e. income that is not pegged on the number of writers and hours that we put to develop our products.

Thanks to my vast experience and dedication to get things done, I am committed to building a six figure passive income publishing business.

To make sure you are part of this journey, I am inviting you to subscribe to our newsletter (http://bit.ly/2fanton6figprogress) to know my progress as far as passive income generation is concerned. That's not all; if making passive income, just like me, is something you'd love to venture into, you can follow my 'tell it all' blog, which

I explain everything I have done to promote every book and how the results are turning out with figures and images.

My goal is to make sure that while I add value to my audience through the different topics that I publish about to solve various problems for instance, I also add massive value to readers in ways that go beyond just one book. Subscribe to our newsletter to know when I publish new books, how I did market research, how I make money with the books and much, much more.

You can even ask questions on anything you want me to answer regarding publishing and everything else related to the topics of discussion.

Antony

Website: http://www.fantonpublishers.com/

Email: Support@fantonpublishers.com

Twitter: https://twitter.com/FantonPublisher

Facebook **Page**: https://www.facebook.com/Fantonpublisher/

My Ketogenic Diet Books Page: https://www.facebook.com/pg/Fast-Keto-Meals-336338180266944

Private Facebook Group For Readers: https://www.facebook.com/groups/FantonPublishers/

Pinterest: https://www.pinterest.com/fantonpublisher/

I look forward to hearing from you!

PSS: Let Me Also Help You Save Some Money!

If you are a heavy reader, have you considered subscribing to Kindle Unlimited? You can read this and millions of other books for just $9.99 a month)! You can check it out by searching for Kindle Unlimited on Amazon!

15328067R00039

Printed in Great Britain
by Amazon